A SENTIMENTAL CHRISTMAS

ISBN 978-1-5400-2914-0

Contact Us:
Hal Leonard
7777 West Bluemound Road
Milwaukee, WI 53213
Email: info@halleonard.com

In Europe contact:
Hal Leonard Europe Limited
Distribution Centre, Newmarket Road
Bury St Edmunds, Suffolk, IP33 3YB
Email: info@halleonardeurope.com

In Australia contact:
Hal Leonard Australia Pty. Ltd.
4 Lentara Court
Cheltenham, Victoria, 3192 Australia
Email: info@halleonard.com.au

CONTENTS

All I Want for Christmas Is You

Words and Music by Mariah Carey and Walter Afanasieff

First note

Verse
Moderately fast

G

1. I don't want a lot ____ for Christ-mas; there is just one thing ____
2. I won't ask for much ____ this Christ-mas; I won't e-ven wish ____

C

____ I need. ____ And I ____ don't care a-bout ____ the pres - ents
____ for snow. ____ And I, ____ I'm just gon - na ____ keep on wait - ing

Cm6

un - der - neath ____ the Christ - mas tree. ____
un - der - neath ____ the mis - tle - toe. ____

G

I don't need ____ to hang ____ my stock - ing
I won't make ____ a list ____ and send ____ it
(D.S.) I don't want ____ a lot for Christ - mas,

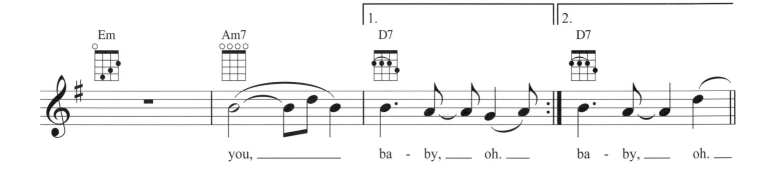

you, _____ ba - by, ___ oh. ___ ba - by, ___ oh. ___

Bridge

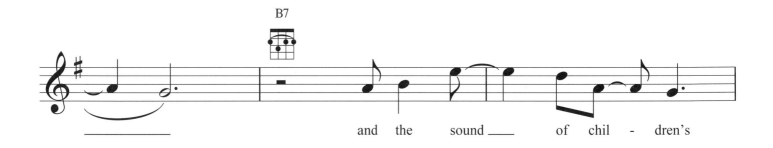

___ All the lights ___ are shin - ing so bright - ly ev - 'ry - where, ___

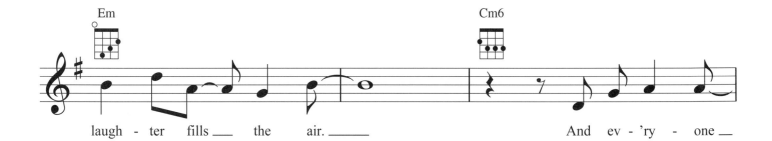

_____ and the sound ___ of chil - dren's

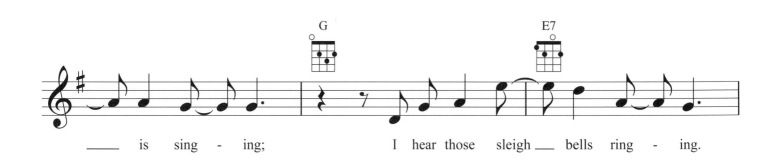

laugh - ter fills ___ the air. _____ And ev - 'ry - one ___

___ is sing - ing; I hear those sleigh ___ bells ring - ing.

San - ta, won't you please bring me what I real - ly need? Won't you

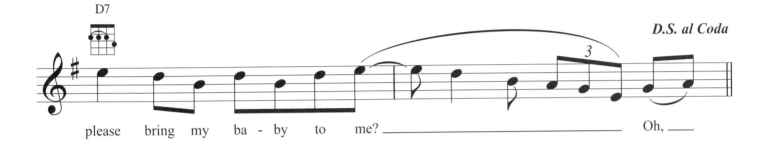

D.S. al Coda

please bring my ba - by to me? _____ Oh, ___

Coda

Christ - mas _____ is _____

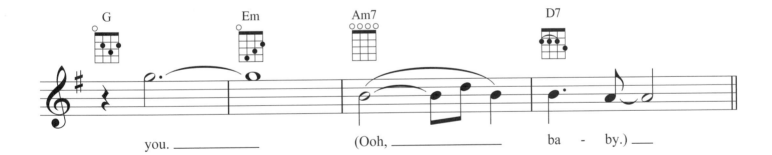

you. _____ (Ooh, ___ ba - by.) ___

Outro

Repeat and fade

All I want for Christ - mas is you, _____ ba - by. ___

Blue Christmas

Words and Music by Billy Hayes and Jay Johnson

you're   not   here   with   me. _____ I'll   have   a   blue

Christ - mas;   that's   cer - tain. _____ And   when   that

blue   heart - ache   starts   hurt - in', _____

_____ you'll   be   do - in'   all   right   with   your

Christ - mas   of   white,   but   I'll   have   a

blue,   blue   Christ - mas. _____

Christmas Lights

**Words and Music by Guy Berryman, Will Champion,
Chris Martin and Jonny Buckland**

First note
× ××

**Verse
Moderately**

G

C   D   G

1. Christ - mas night,   an - oth - er fight.   Tears we cried,   a flood. ___
(2.) took   my   feet   to   Ox - ford Street,   tryin' to right   a wrong. ___

___   Got all kinds ___ of poi - son in,   of
___   "Just   walk a - way," ___ those win - dows say,   but I

1.
Csus2   Dsus4
3fr

2.
Csus2   Dsus4
3fr

poi - son in _____ my blood. ___   2. I
can't be - lieve ___ she's gone. ___   When

Pre-Chorus

Csus2
3fr

you're still wait - ing for the snow to fall, ___ it does - n't real - ly feel like

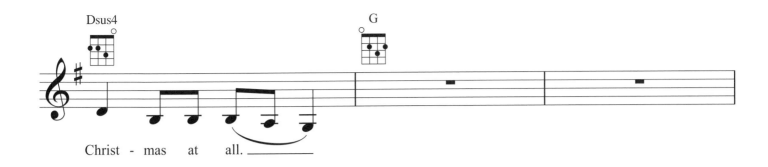

Christ - mas at all. _____

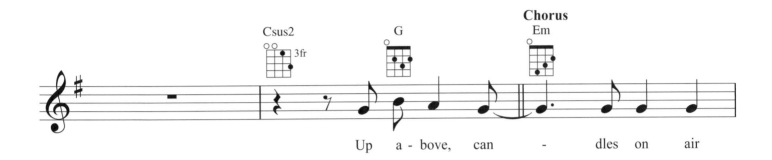

Chorus

Up a - bove, can - dles on air

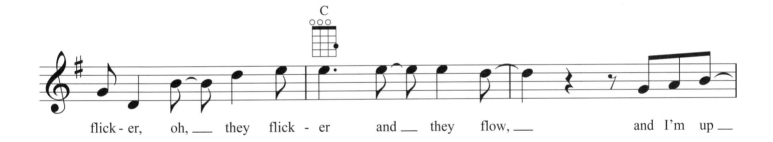

flick - er, oh, __ they flick - er and __ they flow, __ and I'm up __

__ here hold - ing on ____ to all __ those chan - de -liers of hope. __

__ Like some drunk - ard in __ this cit - y, I __ go

sing - ing out of tune, _____ sing - ing how _____ I al - ways loved _

_____ you, dar - ling, and _____ I al - ways will. _____ Oh, when you're _

Pre-Chorus

_____ still wait - ing for the snow to fall, _____ it does - n't real - ly feel like

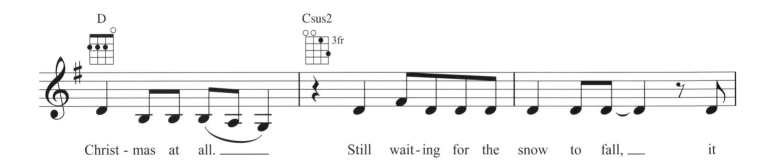

Christ - mas at all. _____ Still wait - ing for the snow to fall, _____ it

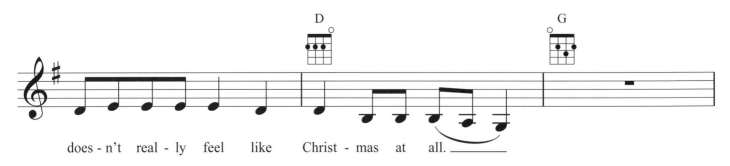

does - n't real - ly feel like Christ - mas at all. _____

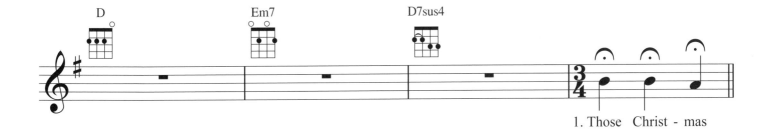

The Christmas Shoes

Words and Music by Leonard Ahlstrom and Eddie Carswell

Pre-Chorus

And his clothes were worn and old, ___ he was dirt-y from head to toe. ___

___ But when it came ___ his time ___ to pay, ___ I

could-n't be-lieve ___ what I heard him say. "Sir, I wan-na

Chorus

buy these shoes ___ for my ma-ma, please. ___ It's

Christ-mas Eve ___ and these shoes are just her ___ size. Could you

hur-ry, sir? ___ Dad-dy says there's not much time. ___ You see,

she's been sick for quite ___ a while, ___ and I know these shoes will make ___

___ her smile, ___ and I want her to look beau - ti - ful ___ if

To Coda ⊕ 1.

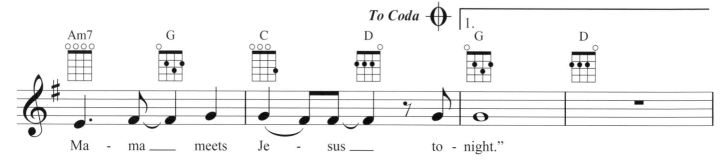

Ma - ma ___ meets Je - sus ___ to - night."

2.

2. They count - ed night." _____ I knew I

Bridge

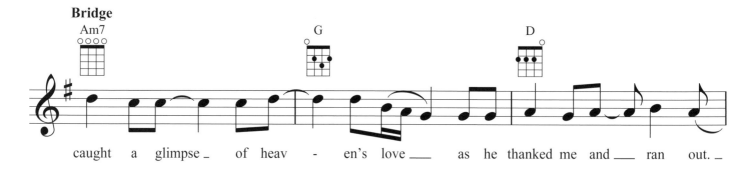

caught a glimpse ___ of heav - en's love ___ as he thanked me and ___ ran out. ___

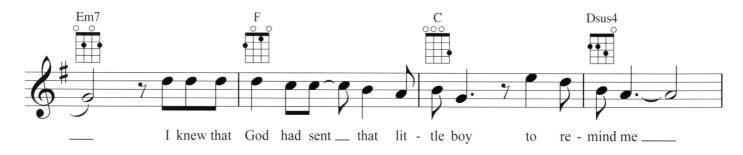

___ I knew that God had sent ___ that lit - tle boy to re - mind me ___

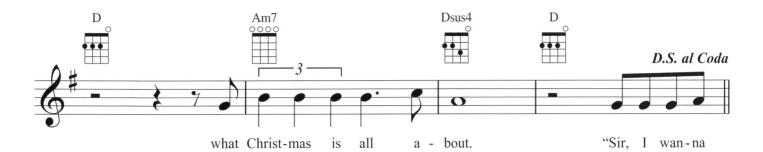

what Christ-mas is all a - bout. "Sir, I wan-na

night. I want her to ____ look beau-

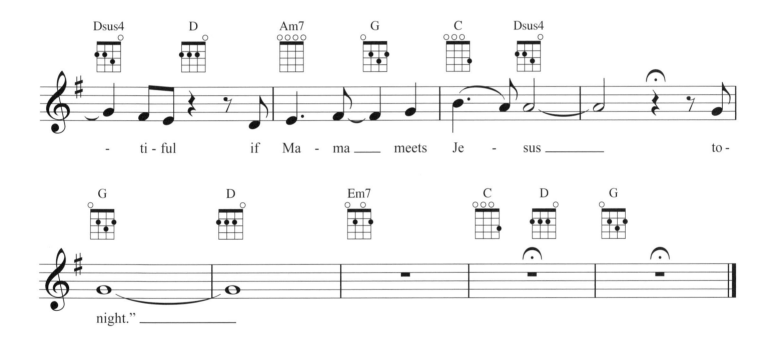

- ti - ful if Ma - ma ____ meets Je - sus ____ to-

night." ____

Additional Lyrics

2. They counted pennies for what seemed like years,
   Then the cashier said, "Son, there's not enough here."
   He searched his pockets frantically,
   Then he turned and he looked at me.
   He said, "Mama made Christmas good at our house,
   Though most years she just did without.
   Tell me, sir, what am I gonna do?
   Somehow I've gotta buy her these Christmas shoes.

Pre-Chorus: So, I laid the money down. I just had to help him out.
   And I'll never forget the look on his face when he said,
   "Mama's gonna look so great."

The Christmas Song
(Chestnuts Roasting on an Open Fire)

Music and Lyric by Mel Tormé and Robert Wells

Christmases When You Were Mine

Words and Music by Nathan Chapman, Liz Rose and Taylor Swift

1. Please take down the mis - tle - toe, _____ 'cause I don't wan - na think a - bout that _____ right now, _____ 'cause ev - 'ry - thing I want is miles _____ a - way _____ in a snow - cov - ered lit - tle town.

2. My ma - ma's in the kitch - en wor - ry - in' a - bout _____ me.
3. I've been do - in' fine with - out _____ you, real - ly,
(4.) bet you got your mom an - oth - er sweat - er.

Sea-son's greet-ings, hope you're well.
up un-til the nights got cold.
Were your cous-ins late a-gain?

Well, I'm do-in' al-right if you ___
And ev-'ry-bod-y's here ex-cept ___
When you were put-tin' up the lights ___

___ were won-der-in'.
___ you, ba - by.
___ this year, _____

Late-ly I can nev-er tell.
Seems like ev-'ry-one's got some-one to
did you no-tice one less pair of hands?

hold.

I know this should-n't be a lone-ly _____
But for me, it's just a lone-ly _____
I know this should-n't be a lone-ly _____

To Coda ⊕

___ time,
___ time,
___ time,

but there were Christ-mas-es when you were
'cause there were Christ-mas-es when you were
but there were

1.

mine.

2.

mine.

Christmas Time Is Here

from *A CHARLIE BROWN CHRISTMAS*
Words by Lee Mendelson
Music by Vince Guaraldi

Fairytale of New York

Words and Music by Jeremy Finer and Shane MacGowan

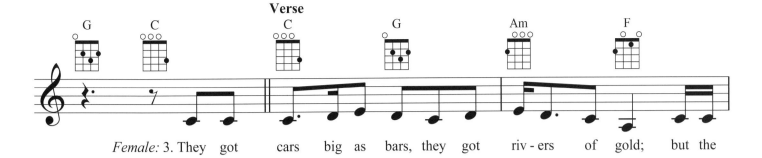

Female: 3. They got cars big as bars, they got riv-ers of gold; but the

wind goes right through you, it's no place for the old. __ When you first took my hand on a cold __

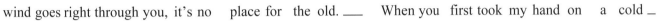

__ Christ-mas Eve, you prom-ised me Broad-way was wait-ing for me. __ 4. You were

Verse

Male: hand-some. You were pret-ty, Queen of New York Cit-y. *Both:* When the band fin-ished play-ing, they
(5.) *See additional lyrics*

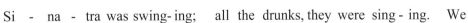

howled out for more. _ Si-na-tra was swing-ing; all the drunks, they were sing-ing. We

Chorus

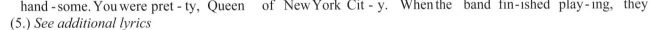
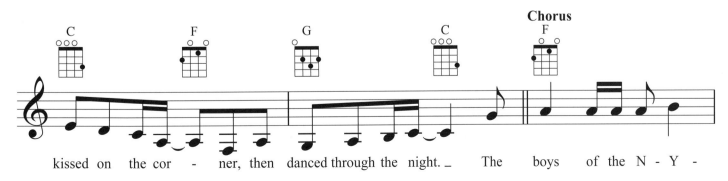

kissed on the cor-ner, then danced through the night. __ The boys of the N - Y -

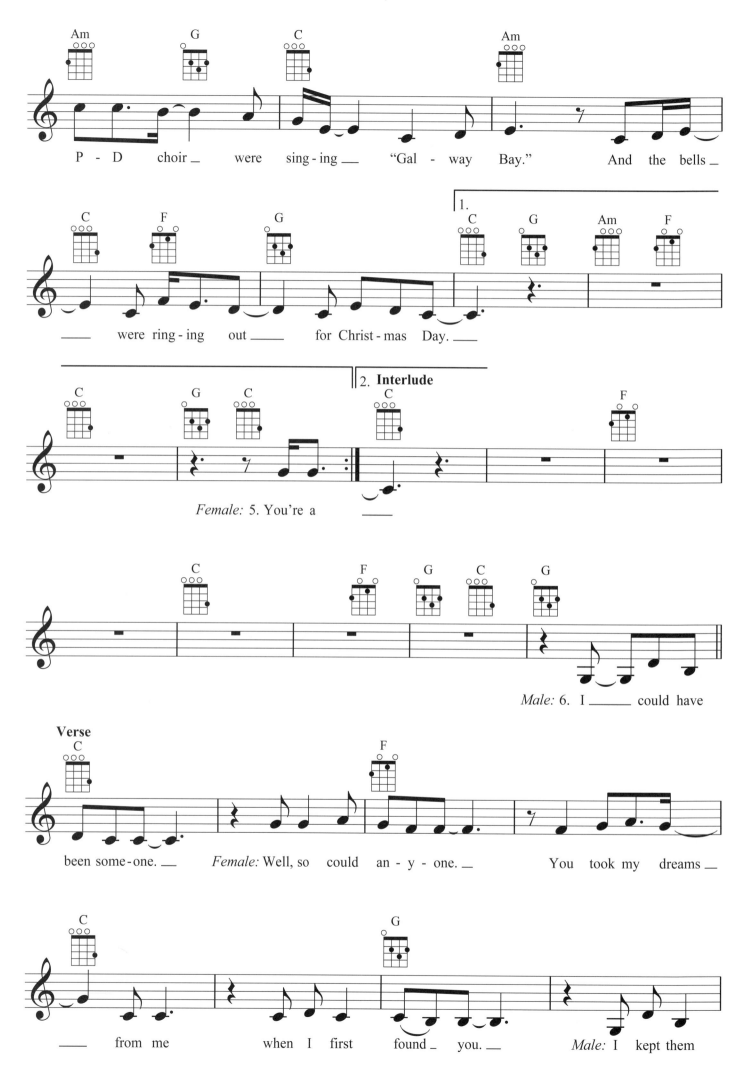

with me, babe; _ I put them with my own. _ Can't _ make it

all a - lone; _ I've built _ my dreams a - round you.

Outro-Chorus

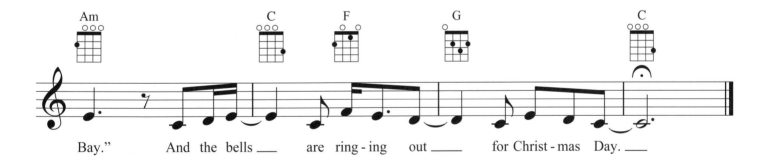

The boys of the N - Y - P - D choir _ still sing - ing _ "Gal - way

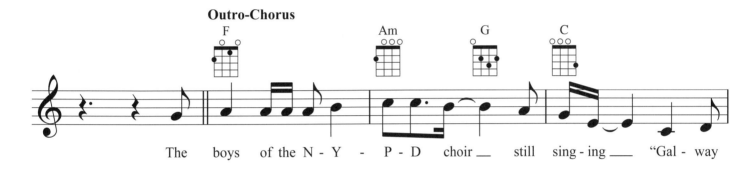

Bay." And the bells _ are ring - ing out _ for Christ - mas Day. _

Additional Lyrics

2. Got on a lucky one, came in eighteen to one;
   I've got a feeling this year's for me and you.
   So happy Christmas; I love you, baby.
   I can see a better time when all our dreams come true.

5. *(Female)* You're a bum, you're a punk!
   (Male) You're an old slut on junk,
   Lying there almost dead on a drip in that bed!
   (Female) You scumbag! You maggot!
   You cheap, lousy faggot!
   Happy Christmas, your arse!
   I pray God it's our last.

Happy Xmas
(War Is Over)

Written by John Lennon and Yoko Ono

Additional Lyrics

2. And so, this is Xmas for weak and for strong,
   The rich and the poor ones; the road is so long.
   And so, happy Xmas for black and for white,
   For the yellow and red ones; let's stop all the fights.

3. And so, this is Xmas, and what have we done?
   Another year over, a new one just begun.
   And so, happy Xmas; we hope you have fun,
   The near and the dear ones, the old and the young.

Have Yourself a Merry Little Christmas

from MEET ME IN ST. LOUIS
Words and Music by Hugh Martin and Ralph Blane

Outro-Verse

(There's No Place Like)
Home for the Holidays

Words and Music by Al Stillman and Robert Allen

I Heard the Bells on Christmas Day

Words by Henry Wadsworth Longfellow
Adapted by Johnny Marks
Music by Johnny Marks

Grown-Up Christmas List

Words and Music by David Foster and Linda Thompson-Jenner

First note

Verse
Moderately slow

1. Do you re-mem-ber me? I sat up-on ___ your knee. ___ I

wrote to you with child - hood fan - ta - sies. 2. Well,

Verse

I'm all grown ___ up now and still need help some - how. I'm
(3.) chil-dren, we ___ be - lieved the grand - est sight to see was

not a child, ___ but my heart still can dream. So,
some - thing love - ly wrapped be - neath our tree. Well,

here's my life - long wish, my grown - up Christ - mas list, not
heav - en sure - ly knows that pack - ag - es and bows can

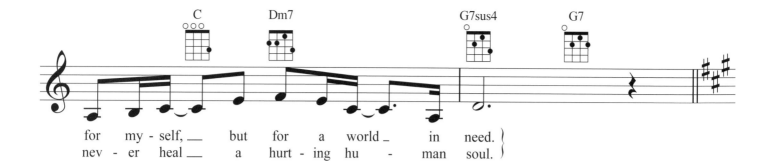

for my - self, ___ but for a world ___ in need.
nev - er heal ___ a hurt - ing hu - man soul.

%. Chorus

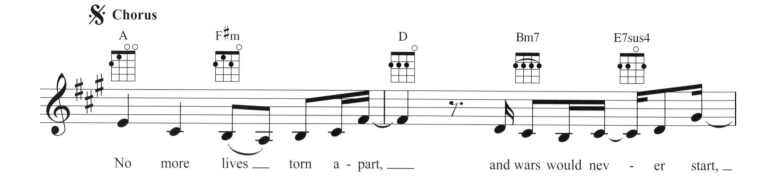

No more lives ___ torn a - part, ___ and wars would nev - er start, ___

___ and time would heal ___ all hearts.

And ev - 'ry - one would have ___ a friend, ___ and right would al - ways

win, and love would nev - er end. ___

This is my grown - up Christ - mas list.

3. As   list. _____

Bridge

What is ____ this il - lu - sion called? The in - no-cence of youth. _ May - be

on - ly in ____ our blind be - lief ____ can we ev - er find _ the truth.

Coda

list. _____

I Wish It Could Be Christmas All Year Long

Words and Music by Phil Baron

I wish it could __ be Christ-mas all year

1. long.

2. Now,

2. I

Bridge

wish that ev - 'ry spir - it in the world __ could feel the pow-

- er and know love, not once a year, __ but ev - 'ry

Verse

min - ute, ev - 'ry ho - ur. __ 3. It's a dream, and

though it seems __ you've heard __ these words be -

fore, it's not a new i - de - a to

wish for some - thing more. ___ But if each day ___ could

feel this way, ___ I know it is - n't wrong. _

_____ I wish it could _ be Christ - mas all year

long. I wish it could _ be

Christ - mas all year long. _____

It Must Have Been the Mistletoe
(Our First Christmas)

Words and Music by Justin Wilde and Doug Konecky

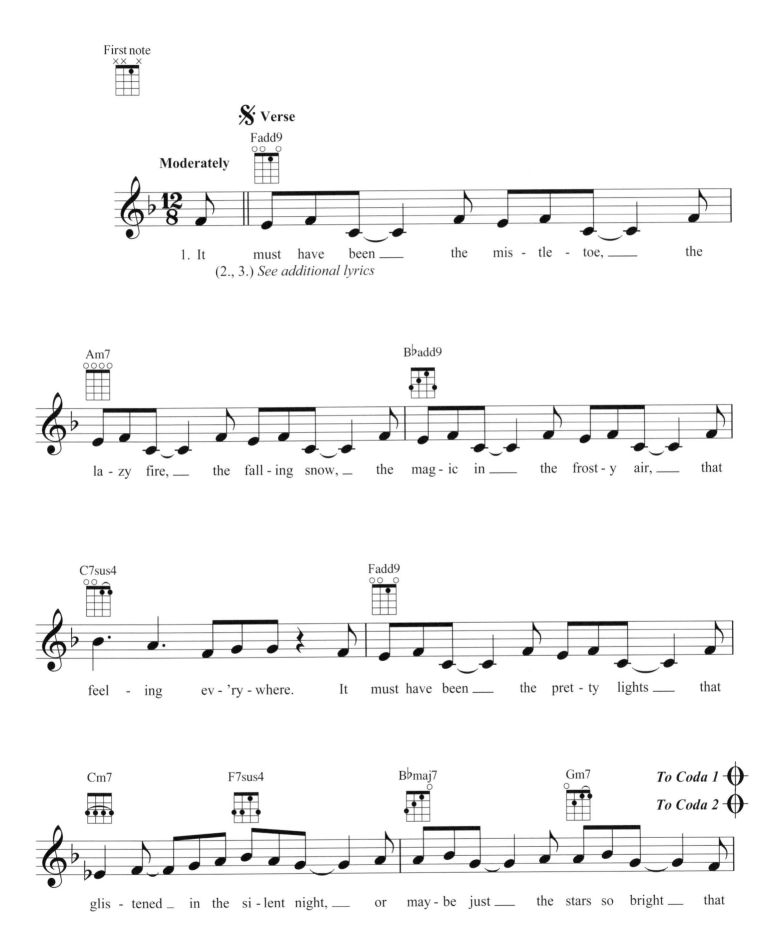

Additional Lyrics

2. It could have been the holiday, the midnight ride upon a sleigh,
   The countryside all dressed in white, that crazy snowball fight.
   It could have been the steeple bell that wrapped us up within its spell.
   It only took one kiss to know; it must have been the mistletoe.

3. It must have been the mistletoe, the lazy fire, the falling snow,
   The magic in the frosty air that made me love you.
   On Christmas Eve a wish came true that night I fell in love with you.
   It only took one kiss to know; it must have been the mistletoe.

I'll Be Home for Christmas

Words and Music by Kim Gannon and Walter Kent

First note

Chorus
Slowly, in 2

I'll   be   home   for   Christ - mas. _____

_____   You   can   plan   on

me. _____   Please   have

snow   and   mis - tle - toe   and

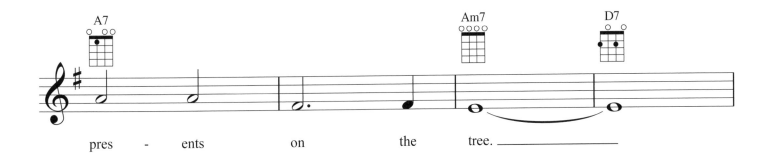

pres - ents on the tree. _____

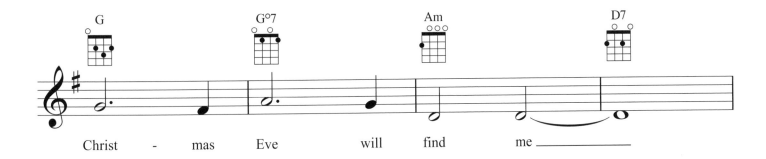

Christ - mas Eve will find me _____

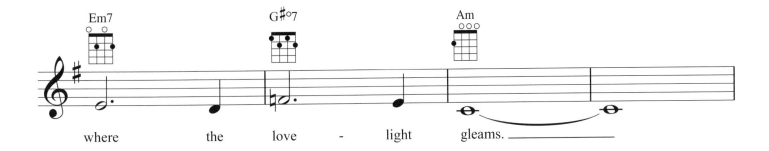

where the love - light gleams. _____

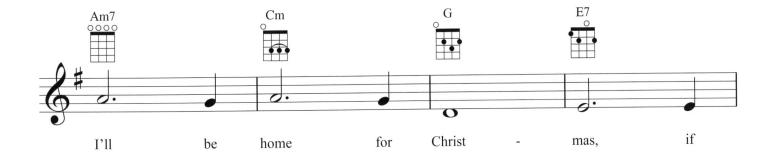

I'll be home for Christ - mas, if

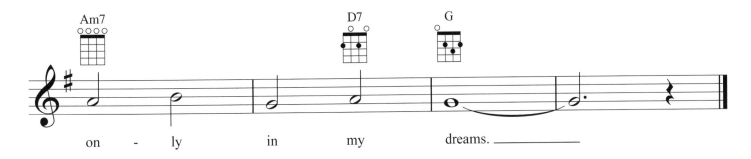

on - ly in my dreams. _____

One Little Christmas Tree

Words and Music by Ronald N. Miller and Bryan Wells

Please Come Home for Christmas

Words and Music by Charles Brown and Gene Redd

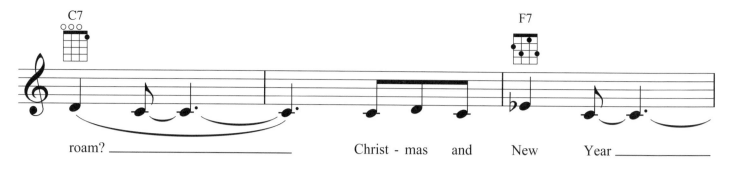

roam? _____ Christ - mas and New Year _____

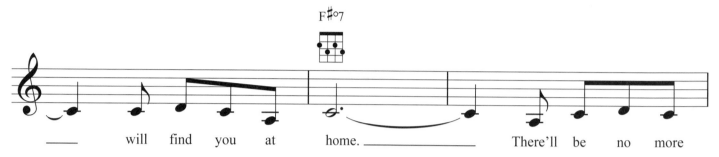

_____ will find you at home. _____ There'll be no more

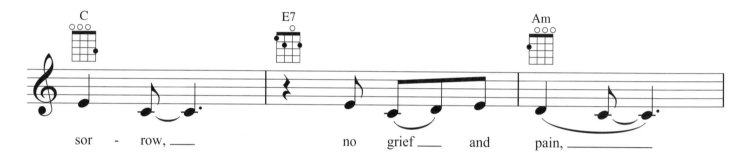

sor - row, ____ no grief ____ and pain, _____

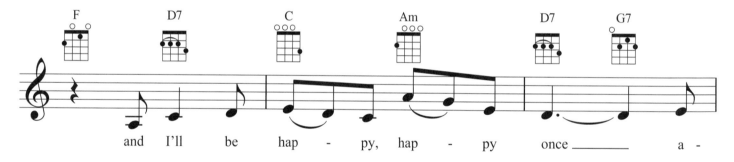

and I'll be hap - py, hap - py once _____ a -

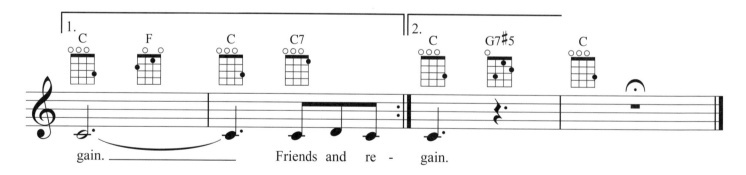

gain. _____ Friends and re - gain.

Additional Lyrics

2. Choirs will be singing "Silent Night,"
   Christmas carols by candlelight.
   Please come home for Christmas,
   Please come home for Christmas.
   If not for Christmas, by New Year's night.

Merry Christmas, Darling

Words and Music by Richard Carpenter and Frank Pooler

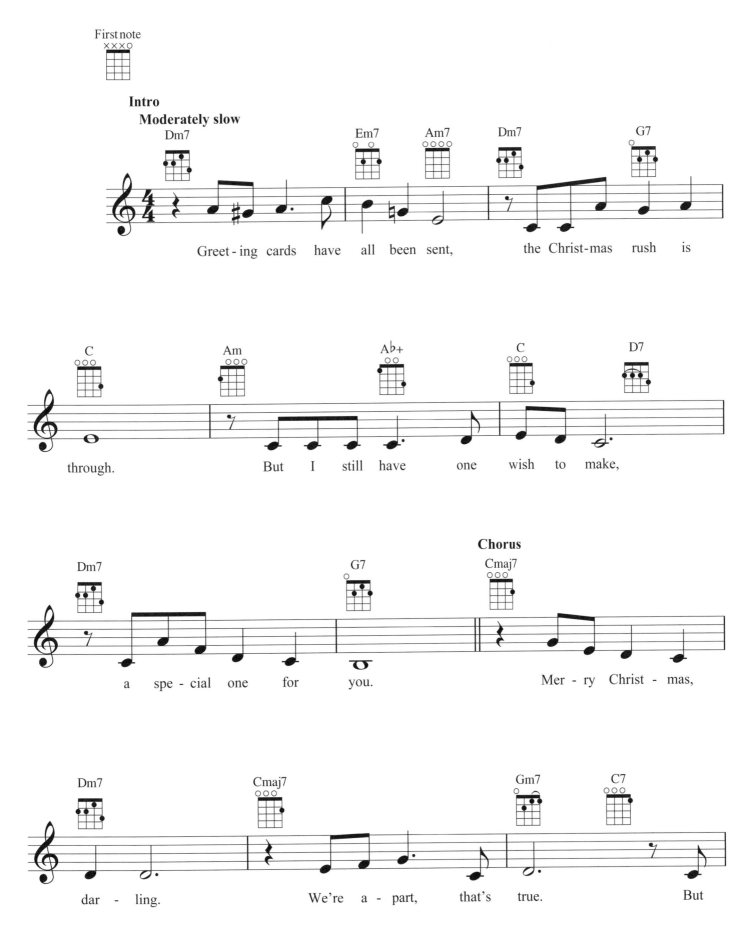

I can dream, and in my dreams, I'm Christ - mas - ing with

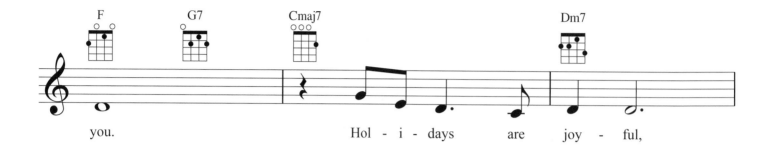

you. Hol - i - days are joy - ful,

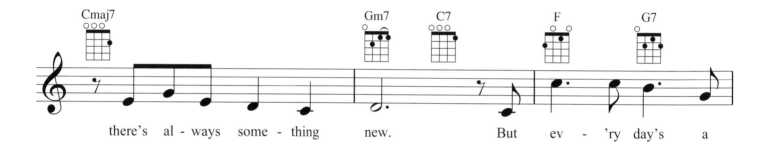

there's al - ways some - thing new. But ev - 'ry day's a

hol - i - day when I'm near to you. The ___

% Bridge

lights on my tree I wish you could see, I wish it ev - 'ry

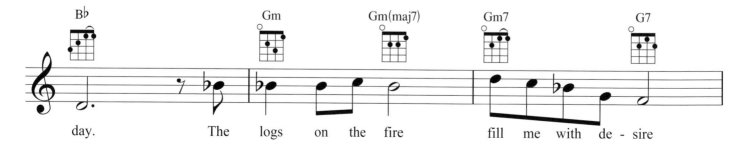

day. The logs on the fire fill me with de - sire

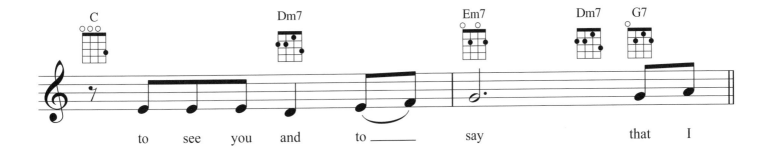

to see you and to _____ say that I

Outro-Chorus

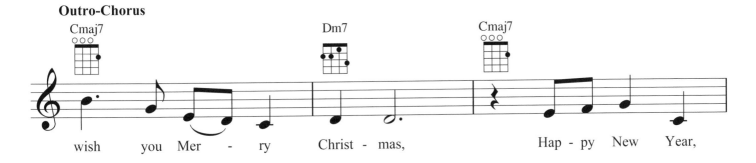

wish you Mer - ry Christ - mas,   Hap - py New Year,

To Coda ⊕

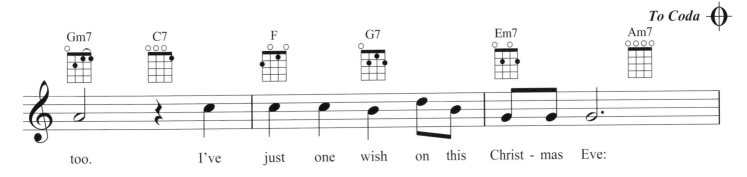

too.   I've just one wish on this Christ - mas Eve:

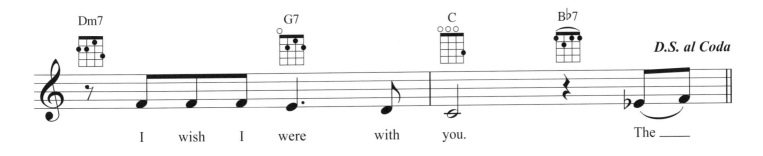

I wish I were with you.   The _____

⊕ **Coda**

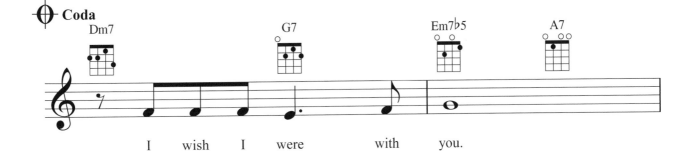

I wish I were with you.

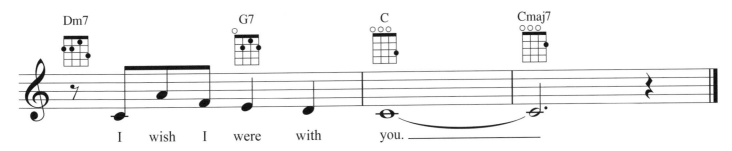

I wish I were with you. _____

Same Old Lang Syne

Words and Music by Dan Fogelberg

Chorus

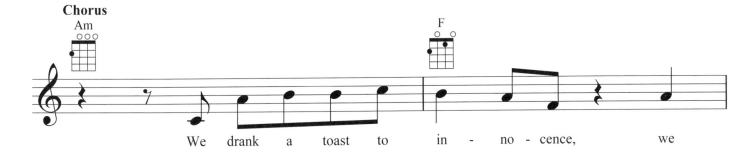

We drank a toast to in - no - cence, we

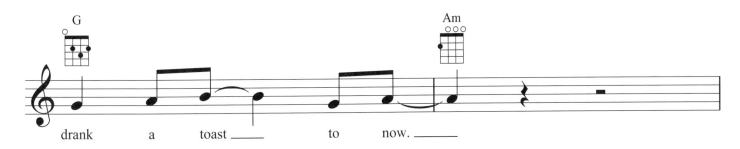

drank a toast ___ to now. ___

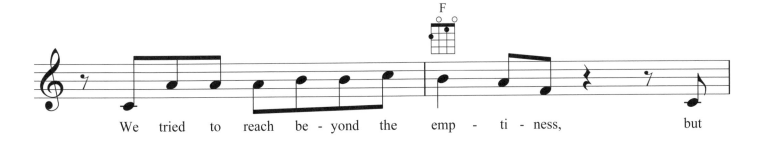

We tried to reach be - yond the emp - ti - ness, but

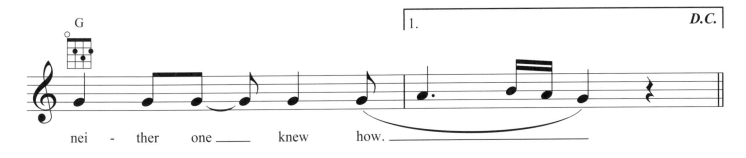

nei - ther one ___ knew how. ___

Chorus

We drank a toast to in - no - cence, we ___

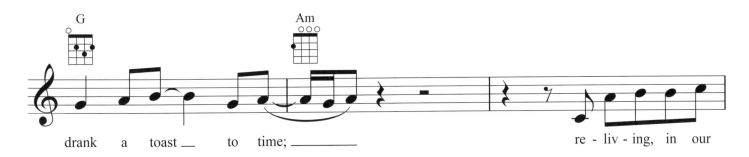

drank a toast ___ to time; ___ re - liv - ing, in our

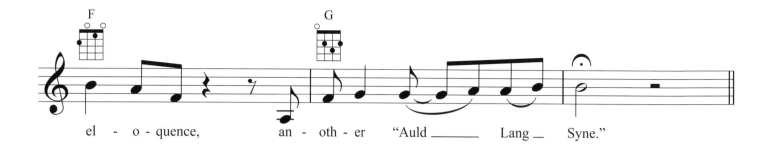

el - o - quence,   an - oth - er "Auld _____ Lang __ Syne."

Verse

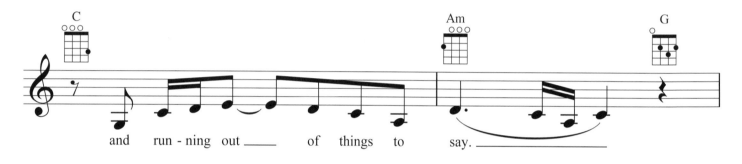

9. The beer was emp - ty and our tongues were tired, _____

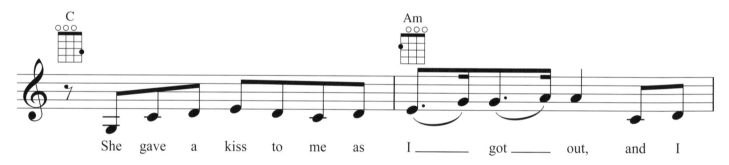

and run - ning out _____ of things to say. _____

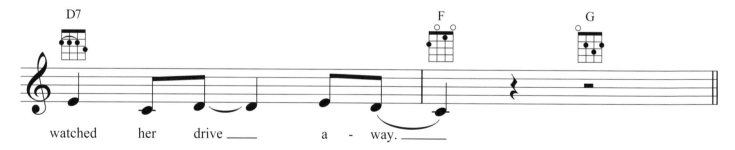

She gave a kiss to me as I _____ got _____ out, and I

watched her drive _____ a - way. _____

Verse
Freely

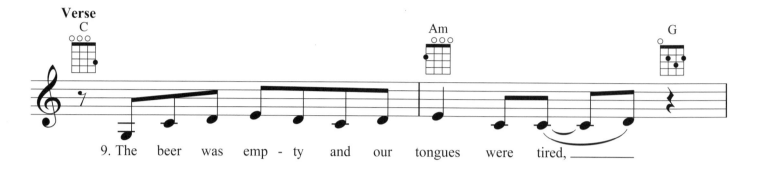

10. Just for a mo - ment I was back at school,

Additional Lyrics

4. We took her groceries to the checkout stand;
   The food was totalled up and bagged.
   We stood there, lost in our embarrassment,
   As the conversation dragged.

5. We went to have ourselves a drink or two,
   But couldn't find an open bar.
   We bought a sixpack at the liquor store
   And we drank it in her car.

6. She said she's married her an architect,
   Who kept her warm and safe and dry.
   She would have liked to say she loved the man,
   But she didn't like to lie.

7. I said the years had been a friend to her
   And that her eyes were still as blue.
   But in those eyes I wasn't sure if I
   Saw doubt or gratitude.

8. She said she saw me in the record stores,
   And that I must be doing well.
   I said the audience was heavenly,
   But the traveling was hell.

Silver Bells

from the Paramount Picture THE LEMON DROP KID
Words and Music by Jay Livingston and Ray Evans

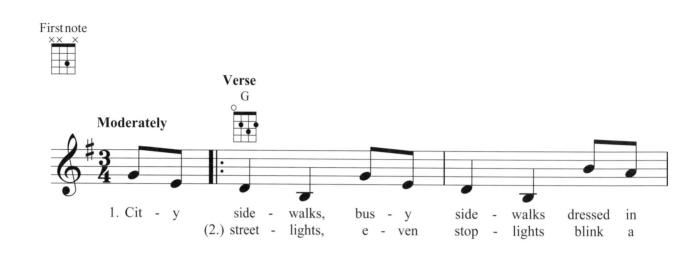

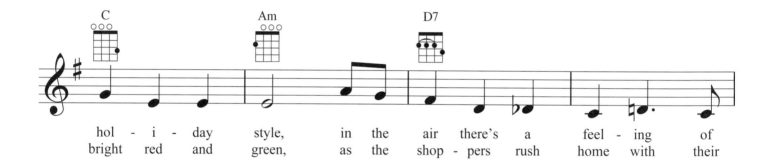

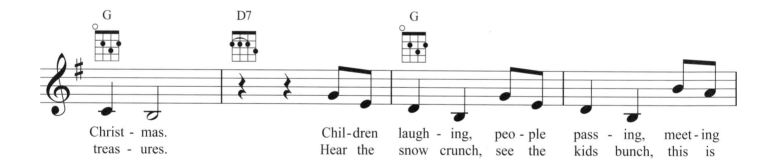

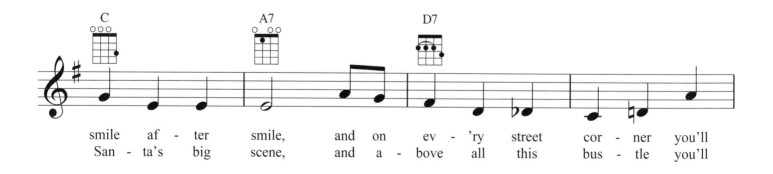

Somewhere in My Memory

from the Twentieth Century Fox Motion Picture HOME ALONE
Words by Leslie Bricusse
Music by John Williams

Tennessee Christmas

Words and Music by Amy Grant and Gary Chapman

Some - bod - y said ___ it's four ___ feet ___ deep. ___ But
Bring home a tan ___ for New ___ Year's ___ Eve. ___

it does - n't mat - ter; give me the laugh - ter.
Sure sounds ex - cit - ing, aw - f'lly in - vit - ing.

I'm gon - na choose ___ to ___ keep ___)
Still, I think I'm ___ gon - na keep ___)   an - oth - er

Chorus

ten - der Ten - nes - see Christ - mas, the

on - ly Christ - mas for me. Where the love cir - cles a - round ___

___ us like the gifts ___ a - round ___ our tree. ___ { Well, I know ___
{ Well, they say ___

62

There's Still My Joy

Words and Music by Melissa Manchester, Matt Rollings and Beth Chapman

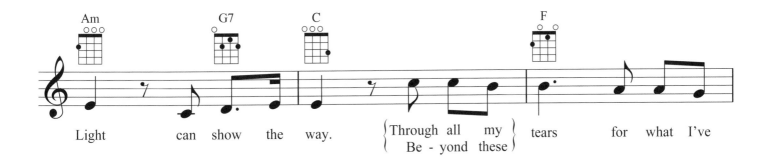

Light can show the way. {Through all my / Be - yond these} tears for what I've

lost, there's still my joy, there's still my joy for Christ - mas

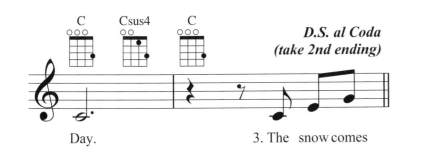

Day.

D.S. al Coda
(take 2nd ending)

3. The snow comes

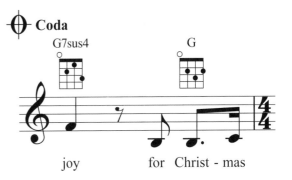

joy for Christ - mas

Day.

Outro

There's still my joy for Christ-mas Day.

White Christmas

from the Motion Picture Irving Berlin's HOLIDAY INN
Words and Music by Irving Berlin

First note
×××○

Chorus
Moderately slow, in 2

I'm   dream - ing   of   a   white

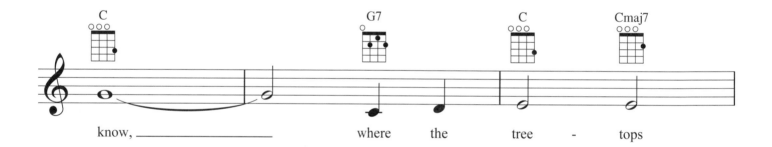

Christ - mas,   just   like   the   ones   I   used   to

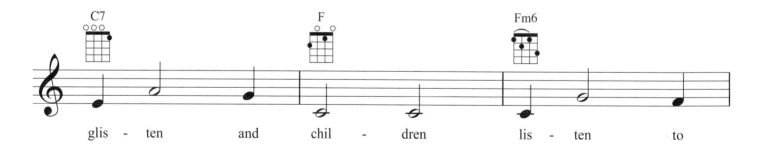

know, _____   where   the   tree - tops

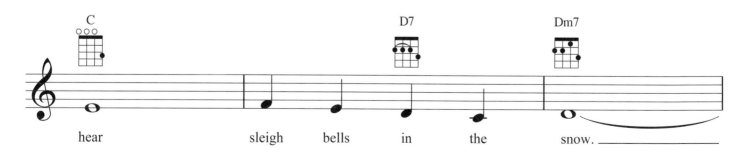

glis - ten   and   chil - dren   lis - ten   to

hear   sleigh   bells   in   the   snow. _____

_____ I'm   dream - ing   of   a_

white   Christ - mas   with   ev - 'ry

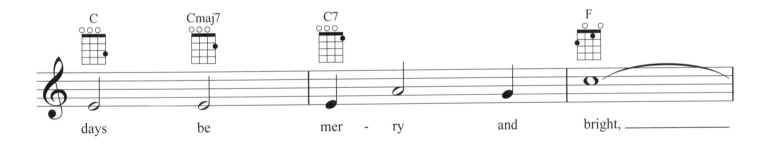

_Christ - mas   card   I   write: _____   "May   your_

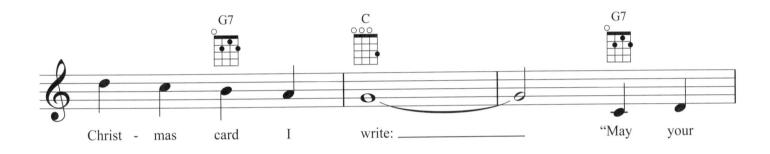

_days   be   mer - ry   and   bright, _____

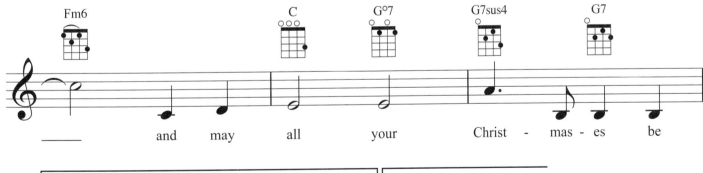

_____   and   may   all   your   Christ - mas - es   be_

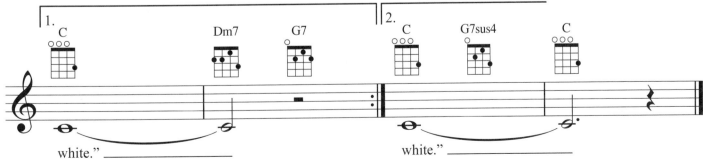

_white." _____   white." _____

You're All I Want for Christmas

Words and Music by Glen Moore and Seger Ellis

Where Are You Christmas?

from Dr. Seuss' HOW THE GRINCH STOLE CHRISTMAS
Words and Music by Will Jennings, James Horner and Mariah Carey

First note

Verse
Gently, in 2

1. Where are you, Christ - mas? Why can't I find you?
4. I feel you, Christ - mas. I know I find found you.

Why have you gone a - way?
You nev - er fade a - way.

Verse

2. Where is the laugh - ter you used to bring me?
3. Where are you, Christ - mas? Do you re - mem - ber
5. The joy of Christ - mas stays here in - side us,

To Coda

Why can't I hear mu - sic play?
the one you used to know?
fills each and ev - 'ry

My world is chang - ing.
I'm not the same one.

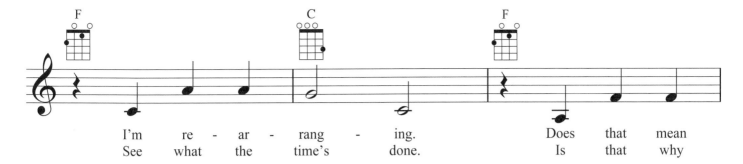

I'm re - ar - rang - ing. Does that mean
See what the time's done. Is that why

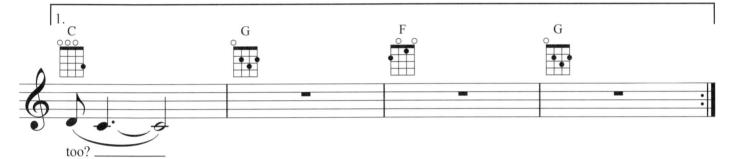

Christ - mas chang - es
you have let me

1.
too?

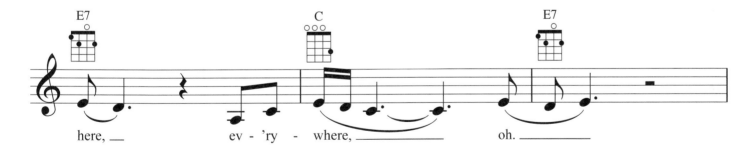

2.
go? Oh. Christ - mas is

Bridge

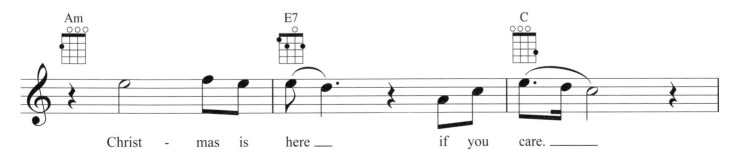

here, ev - 'ry - where, oh.

Christ - mas is here if you care.

If there is love ___ in your

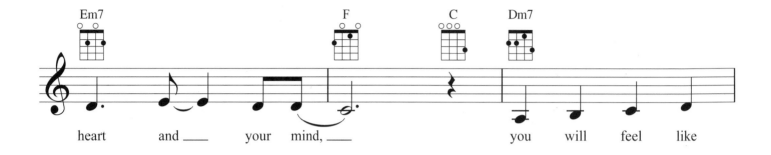

heart and ___ your mind, ___ you will feel like

Christ - mas all the time. ___

D.C. al Coda

Coda

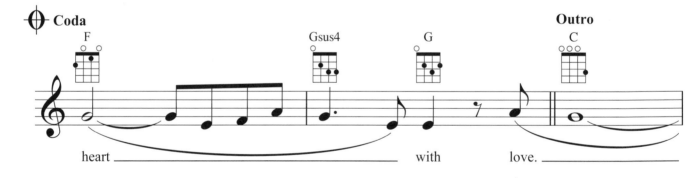

heart ___ with love. ___

Outro

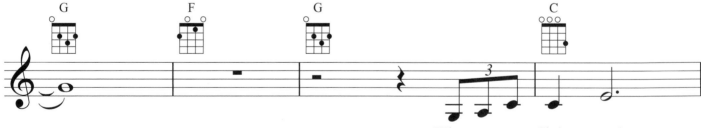

___ Where are you, Christ - mas?

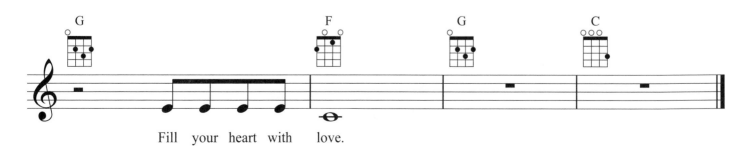

Fill your heart with love.